WINSTON CHURCHILL

A Life of Inspiration

Ryan Patterson

warranties, express or implied, about the completeness, accuracy, reliability, suitability or availability with respect to the information, products, services, or related graphics contained in this book for any purpose.

The trademarks that are used are without any consent, and the publication of the trademark is without permission or backing by the trademark owner. All trademarks and brands within this book are for clarifying purposes only and are owned by the owners themselves, not affiliated with this document.

The author claims no responsibility to any person or entity for any liability, loss or damage caused or alleged to be caused directly or indirectly as a result of the use, application or interpretation of the information presented herein.

Introduction

Keep cool, men! This will be interesting for my paper!

-Winston Churchill, 15 November 1899, as cited by Richard Langworth, Churchill Historian and editor of the book "Churchill: In His Own Words," a collection of Churchill's speeches and quotations

The courtyard surrounding the school building seemed perpetually guarded. Sentries were patrolling the grounds of the girls' school in Pretoria. It had been turned into a prison as the Second Boer War went into full swing.

Three conspirators peered from the window of their confinement onto the courtyard. If one man is fit enough, the wall at the far end of the courtyard could be scaled out. That much the men figured.

In the dead of night, the determined prisoners made their move. Two sentries were seen guarding one wall of the courtyard. Beaded sweat trickled down their temples as they waited. And waited.

Alas! The odds were on their side. The conspirators silently listened as two sentries stopped at one end of the wall and started to converse.

Aided with stealth and agility, the conspirators ran towards a part of the wall unseen to the sentries. While two of the conspirators were unlucky as the sentries became suspicious, one man scaled the wall and into the arms of freedom.

Just days before, after running into an old friend, Captain Haldane, the escaped conspirator eagerly joined a reconnaissance train from Durban to Ladysmith. As the train was ambushed by the Boers midway, the man quipped, "Keep cool, men! This will be interesting for my paper!"

Escaping the Boers during the war in South Africa was one of the most famous – and useful, events in Churchill's life. He made the decision to help the wounded during the ambush, which led to his capture.

Upon returning home six months later, Churchill's words could be heard echoing. While his capture in the Boer war made him world-famous overnight, it also paved the way for his entrance into politics.

It's awe-inspiring how Churchill's life in the military and politics complemented each other through the course of his life. Indeed, the works and achievements of the great, invincible Sir Winston Churchill are all interesting to read – as interesting as his life had been. What's written in his books and everything elsewhere that's about him are largely true. Now, who wouldn't look up to the man?

By the age of 25, he had already become larger than life in his own right. He had already faced combat in South America, Asia, and Africa. During those wars, he won four medals and was accepted in a highly respected order. He published books about his adventures in the wars and became internationally recognized as a result. More importantly, he was elected into the parliament, which started his long, profound career as a statesman.

Churchill's political career solidified his place in today's history books. As an accomplished civil servant, he held many positions in the House of Commons including being one of the greatest prime ministers that UK has had. Among his other most notable services were as First Lord of the Admiralty, Minister of Munitions, and Chancellor of the Exchequer.

While historians and biographers hailed Churchill as "the greatest statesman of the 20th century", he was also known as an orator, war correspondent, journalist, Nobel Prize winner, and author. In private life, he is known to his family as an avid reader, historian, animal-lover, and painter.

However, everything did not always go well in Churchill's life.

The Gallipoli disaster in Turkey forced him to resign as Lord of the Admiralty. While Chancellor of Exchequer at one point, his decision to reintroduce the Gold Standard raised unemployment rate and caused a nationwide negative inflation rate. Most notably, his efforts to retain his seat as PM after WWII defeated him inside. In his private life meanwhile, Churchill fought a lifelong battle against depression.

How would he have become the Greatest Briton after all these and with a lifelong depression to boot? This, you have to find out.

Everybody knows Churchill for his cigar, "V" sign, ambitious stride, and bulldog scowl. Through this book however, you will understand and see a complete picture of Churchill's private and public life – and how he became the Greatest Briton of Modern History.

Table of Contents

Chapter 1

✄ EARLY LIFE AND FAMILY HISTORY ✄

In all our long history, we have never seen a greater day than this.

-Winston Churchill, May 1945

*I*n a Victorian room on the ground floor of the Blenheim Palace, away from the tapestried saloons and state apartments, Winston Leonard Spencer Churchill was born on the 30th of November 1874 in Woodstock, Oxfordshire, England. Lady Randolph, Churchill's mother, was on a visit to the palace when she accidentally fell, which induced labor and led to Winston's premature birth just shy of 2 months.

Born to a wealthy aristocratic family, he experienced the life that other rich Victorian era boys were often led into. While his parents were socially and politically active, they had no time for the little Churchill. Like the wealthy ladies of her time, Lady Randolph hired a nanny to look after her child. It was in February 1875 then, that the devoted Mrs. Elizabeth Ann Everest was hired.

In Mrs. Everest, Winston found the love that he could've otherwise received from his mother, a distant and glamorous figure in his life. He called his nanny "woom", "woomy", or "woomany", which was as close to how he could effectively pronounce "woman" at a young age, especially considering his lisp.

Little Winston grew very close and fond of his "woomany" mainly because of the constant absence of his parents. With limited contact with them, he considered Mrs. Everest not only as his nanny, but as his most trusted confidante and mother substitute. When news of her ill health reached Churchill in 1895, he rushed to her side, and hired a doctor and nurse to look after her. She died of diphtheria in July of that same year with Churchill at her side.

Mrs. Everest's funeral and tombstone, all paid by Churchill despite his meager income back then, lied in the City of London Cemetery (maintained to this day by the UK International Churchill Society) with the inscription, "Erected to the memory of Elizabeth Ann Everest who died on 3rd July 1895 aged 62 years, by Winston Spencer Churchill and John Spencer Churchill."

✿ Family History ✿

Right from the start, expectations were high for the young Winston. Having been born into an aristocratic family, achievements abounded in his family's lineage. He was from the aristocratic family of the Dukedom of Marlborough, a hereditary title given to a member of the vast and noble Spencer family, of which the late Diana, Princess of Wales, was also a member.

The title was first given in 1702 to a war hero, General John Churchill (1650-1722), by Queen Anne (1665-1714), who reigned from 1702 to 1707, for his successful military campaigns across Europe. He was considered to be one of the greatest generals of the European continent, having been able to suppress a rebellion, lead a revolution, and commanded European armies to war (against Louis XIV of France) and winning them. He also helped a few monarchs (Kings James II 1685-1688 and William III 1689-1702 of England) to secure their thrones, aside from Queen Anne.

As life unfolded, marriages between families changed the name of the Dukedom to Spencer. In 1817, the 5th Duke of Marlborough, George Spencer, changed the family name to Spencer-Churchill to indicate that their lineage is of direct descent from the 1st Duke of Marlborough, General John Churchill.

The prominent, though often controversial, Tory (the Conservative and Unionist Party today) politician Lord Randolph Henry Spencer-Churchill, was Winston's father. He was the third and youngest son of John Spencer-Churchill, the 7th Duke of Marlborough. His interest in politics started when he served unofficially as his father's, then Lord Lieutenant (Viceroy) of Ireland, private secretary in Dublin from 1875 to 1880.

Lord Randolph later became the Secretary of State for India 1885-1886, Leader of the House of Commons 1886-1887, and Chancellor of the Exchequer 1886. He was however, best known for advocating Conservative policies that led to the Tory Democracy. Although this new set of views became popular to the rank-and-file representatives of the Tories, it did not do well with the old Conservatives, especially with their leader, Lord Robert Cecil, the 3rd Marquess of Salisbury. Winston's father would've been elected prime minister if not for his political approach and new ideologies.

After his resignation from office in 1886, he spent much of his time attending horse races. He lost interest in politics and succumbed to a tragic and painful death due to general syphilitic paresis in 1895, the same year Winston's nanny, Mrs. Everest, died.

Lord Randolph Henry Spencer-Churchill, Winston's father. (c) BBC Fulton Picture Library via Britannica Online

Unbeknownst to many, Winston's mother was an American, born and bred. The beautiful and widely popular British socialite, Jeannette Jerome, known to her family and friends as Jennie, was born in Brooklyn, New York. She was the daughter of Leonard Jerome and Clarissa Hall. Jerome was a lawyer who became a wealthy financier, and a sports (yachting, horse racing, and hunting) enthusiast. Clarissa on the other hand, better known as Clara to her family and friends, was a socialite.

Jennie's paternal side of her family was already known for their participation during the American Revolution as members of George Washington's armies. However, it was Leonard's intense fascination for sports that earned him two street (Jerome Avenue in the Bronx and Brooklyn) names, a racetrack (Jerome Stakes in Queens), and a park reservoir (Jerome Park Reservoir) all in his home state of New York.

There were obvious reasons as to how and why an American socialite was able to marry a member of a British aristocratic family. First, it was Leonard's fortune that allowed his four daughters to experience a prosperous life in Europe. Second, at the later part of the Victorian age, it was common for wealthy Americans, often heiresses, to live, study, and get married with individuals from noble, aristocratic families in Europe. Such was the case for Lord Randolph and Jennie.

In August 1873, while on a boat race (hosted by Prince Albert Edward, the future King Edward VII) off the coast of the Isle of Wight in England, Lord Randolph and Jennie were introduced to each other by Frank Bertie (who someday would also introduce Lord Randolph's son, Jack to his future wife, Lady Gwendoline). Just three days after their first meeting, an engagement between the two was announced. Less than a year later on the 15th of April 1874, the two were married. Jennie officially became Lady Randolph Churchill.

Lady Randolph was highly supportive of her husband's political career. Using her American wit and cheerfulness, she often served as hostess to many of her husband's political gatherings and even actively campaigned for his agendas. Despite this, their relationship turned sour and stories of infidelities on both sides were often reported.

When Lord Randolph died in 1895, she stayed in England, married again twice, and died in 1921 after falling off the stairs of a friend's house. She did not die because of the fall, but it broke her left ankle which caused gangrene to set in. Her entire left leg had to be amputated. Unfortunately, it caused hemorrhage in a major artery and more than two weeks later, she died on June 29. Like Winston's father, his mother went through a slow, painful death.

Early Childhood

The social and political activities of Winston's parents were seen as the main reason for their neglect of their children. They later had John Strange Spencer-Churchill in 1880 while they lived in Dublin. They often left their children to the care of their nurses and although Winston manifested many of his parents' traits, from his father's political powers to his mother's unique charisma, he grew up distant from them as did his brother John who they fondly called Jack.

Before Jack however, the Churchills initially lived in Blenheim Palace, the official seat (or house) of the Dukes of Marlborough. It was a military honour, as instructed by then Queen Anne, built for the victories of the 1st Duke of Marlborough, General John Churchill. The palace took nearly two decades to finish from 1705 to 1722. In 1987, it was declared as a United Nations World Heritage Site.

When Winston was two years old in 1876, his family moved to Dublin, Ireland where Lord Randolph served as private secretary to his father, John Spencer-Churchill, newly appointed Viceroy of Ireland. Here, a governess was hired to teach Winston basic reading, writing, and simple mathematics.

Young Winston (boy at right) with his younger brother, Jack, and mother, Lady Randolph. (c) Time/Getty Images via Independent UK

As Winston turned six years old, his family returned to England where he received his first private education two years later. In 1882, Winston was admitted to the St. George's School, a private school in Ascot, Berkshire, England, where he studied until 1884. After that, he was admitted to The Misses Thomsons' Preparatory School, owned by sisters Charlotte (1843-1901) and Catherine Amelia (1845-1906), in Brunswick Road, Brighton in East Sussex. The school was by the sea, which Winston finally learned to enjoy.

Winston wasn't exactly happy at St. George. He described and wrote later in life that he saw his first school as an inconvenience. After all, he had all the toys he wanted in the world and he didn't want to be away from them. As a result, the little boy's rebellious, independent character only brought him poor grades in school.

At Misses Thomson's however, he finally saw hope. Here, he learned to swim and ride a horse (with a pony). He also learned French. It was also here that he first learned to love history and poetry.

It was in Harrow School, a boarding school for boys near London, that Winston later admitted he hated schools and lessons. This was according to Sir Shane Leslie (officially Sir Randolph Leslie, 3rd Baronet or Ireland), a first cousin (Sir Shane's mother, Leonie Jerome, and Churchill's mother, Jennie Jerome, were sisters) and lifelong friend of Churchill. He failed miserably in his schoolwork and often lost his books. He was however, interested in Harrow's Rifle Corps and immediately became part of it.

As a Corps member, Winston was able to perfect his horse-riding skills. He learned to fire a rifle and participate in fencing, which he was good at.

He was admitted to Harrow in 1888 in which he often wrote letters to her mother, begging her to visit or let him come home even for a brief stay. Unfortunately, the socialite Lady Randolph rarely visited his son, nor allowed him to visit them at home. On one occasion, Winston had to deliver a speech during Harrow's Speech Day. As usual, his parents were not available for attendance. Mrs. Everest, his beloved nanny, stood in to substitute.

Again, his remote parents' treatment of his school work indirectly returned the young boy's poor academics. The young Winston wanted to see his parents often. Sadly, the Churchills never saw their absence as a contributing factor to their son's poor academic performance. Lord Randolph merely saw his son's interest is solely focused on his toy soldiers. It was during this time, 1889 to be exact, that Lord Randolph believed that his son was meant for military school.

✎ Introduction to Military School ✎

That same year, Churchill's parents decided to enroll Winston in Harrow's army classes to prepare him for the Sandhurst's entrance exam.

After leaving Harrow in 1892, Winston took entrance exams for the Royal Military College (now Academy) in Sandhurst, Berkshire, England. He flunked the entrance exams twice, to the dismay of his father who in a letter said that Winston will become a *"social wastrel"* if he keeps on leading the *"idle, useless, unprofitable life"* he used to have during his early school days.

Many believe that Churchill's haste to accomplish great things at a young age, and later in life, can be attributed to his longing to keep up with his father's ambitions and desires for him. The two rarely spoke to each other and if there was a chance that they did, Lord Randolph simply railed at his son for being a failure in his own eyes.

Fortunately, by Winston's third attempt, he passed the entrance exam for the Royal Military College and entered the school as an officer cadet in September 1893. He was eager to please his father, and was completely interested in military life which started when he was a little boy in Dublin, watching his grandfather's military parades passing by the Vice Regal Lodge (currently the presidential residence in Ireland president and is called the Aras an Uachtarain) where the family used to live.

At Sandhurst, Winston showed his unwavering interest to be a soldier in the cavalry (instead of the infantry). This meant that he was not required to get high grades or learn more about mathematics, a subject which he learned early on but only grew to despise. He loved learning more about the English language instead, which he did vigorously on his own.

The young Winston excelled at Sandhurst. He believed he was destined for the army and started to feel like a real man. He was also starting to impress his father and earn his respect when unfortunately, Lord Randolph died at the young age of 45 in April 1895. Three months later, his dear nanny

Mrs. Everest died, too. Churchill was left devastated by the sudden, tragic turn of events.

Proving he was worthy of his father's respect, Winston passed out (graduated) high with honors more than half a year later in December 1894. From a class of 130 cadets, he was on the top 20. His military life had just begun.

Chapter 2

⚔ LIFE IN THE MILITARY ⚔

This is not the end. It is not even the beginning of the end. But it is, perhaps, the end of the beginning.

-Winston Churchill, November 1942, at the Lord Mayor's Luncheon at Mansion House in London, for the Allied victory in the Second Battle of El Alamein (Egypt)

*W*inston was destined for the army. By the age of 25, his imperial adventures enabled him to have already served in five wars including the Cuban War of Independence, the Mohmand Campaign in India, Battle of Omdurman in Sudan, and the Second Boer War in South Africa. It all started when Winston joined the 4th Queen's Own Hussars in January 1895.

Churchill's entrance exam at Sandhurst resulted in him being 95th out of the 389 examinees. Four places higher and he would've qualified to enter the infantry regiment. However, he decided he might as well stay within the cavalry, instead of the infantry which his father would've wanted. In a letter to his mother in 1894, Winston had expressed early on that he wanted to serve in the cavalry rather than in the "old Rifles" which his father preferred. He went on saying that his physical weakness may prove him unworthy, useless in the infantry. Besides, according to him, *"of all regiments in the army the Rifles is slowest for promotion."*

Winston loved the 4th Hussars. He considered it his home. It was the British Army's cavalry regiment and originally named the Princess Anne of Denmark's Regiment of Dragoons. Brigadier General John Berkeley, 4th Viscount Fitzhardinge (1650-1712), the man tasked to form the necessary troops, was the Master of the Horses (a member of the Royal Household in charge of the King's stables, horses and its breeds, hounds, and all those who work in the King's Stables. Today however, the title is only used for ceremonial purposes.) for then King James II's daughter (and future Queen) Princess Anne, thus the name.

A rebellion was organized and staged by the Protestant James Scott, the Duke of Monmouth (1649-1685), and his supporters against his uncle the Roman Catholic King James II (1633-1701). It was aptly named the Monmouth Rebellion (1685) which saw the failed attempt to overthrow James II. To protect his domain and reign, King James asked the Parliament to grant him funds for forming army troops. In 1685, his request was granted and that was when the Princess Anne of Denmark's Regiment of Dragoons was formed. In 1861, it became the 4th Queen's Own Hussars and served its purpose until 1958. In 1993 however, it was combined with the 8th Queen's Royal Irish Hussars and is now known as the Queen's Royal Hussars (Queen's Own and Royal Irish).

After joining the 4th Hussars, Churchill was commissioned a month later to be a cornet, equivalent to today's second Lieutenant. His first assignment was set to be in India. An assignment he knew, would take longer than expected. However, the assignment would not be in effect until a year later.

Back then, life in a cavalry regiment meant training and maneuvers for seven months during the summer season, followed by five months or more of leave. This worried the newly-issued lieutenant. He had no means of supplementing an aristocratic life while on military leave. He was receiving a yearly allowance of £400 from Lady Randolph, but it wasn't enough.

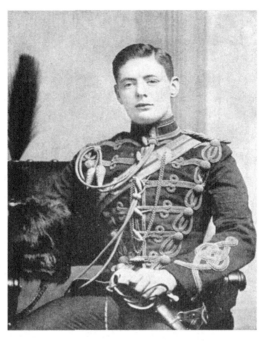

Lieutenant Churchill of the 4th Queen's Own Hussars, 1895. (c) Universal History Archive/Getty Images via Huffington Post UK

Wanting to consider all his options, Winston made calculations of his earnings and expenses. As a new officer, his pay was to be £120 per year. Unfortunately, officers had to pay for their uniforms, horses and equipment which after calculations, amounted to £653. His grandparents already gave him a £200 horse, so he was still more than £300 short. In other words, he had expenses that could only be paid after serving five years in the cavalry.

Apparently, Churchill couldn't wait that long. He had to act immediately if he wanted to solve the predicaments he was facing. Now he had to earn even more money to fund both his aristocratic and military officer lifestyles. He had to create his own opportunities for this to happen.

Roy Jenkins, author of Churchill: A Biography (2001), believed that the only way for Churchill to earn extra money was to work as a war correspondent. This could be true considering that he often mentioned to Lady Randolph through his letters to her that he wanted to be promoted to a higher rank as fast as possible. To do this, he has to be present in numerous military actions instead of following a conventional way of promotion.

However, Churchill's love of the English language could be taken as a more profound reason why he could've wanted to be a war correspondent in the first place. Back when he was just a schoolboy in Harrow, he loved how his English form master (teacher), Robert Somervell (1851-1933), taught the subject. He saw that learning the language was like a kind of drill, something that is entirely in parallel to his interest in military life.

With the help of Lady Randolph and the influence of Churchill's family in high society, he was able to gain permission to participate in the war in Cuba. At the same time, he entered into a contract with the Daily Graphic, a weekly illustrated newspaper. He was finally, all set.

↘ The Cuban War of Independence ↙

Filled with an air of supposed courage, Lieutenant Churchill sailed for Cuba on November 1985, just a few months after Lord Randolph, his equally impulsive father, died. For the next couple of weeks, his mission was to provide news of guerilla warfare between the Cubans and its colonizers, the Spaniards, to Daily Graphic. The Cubans wanted independence from Spain. In 1898, they won with the intervention of the United States which led to the Spanish-American War (April–August 1898).

Meanwhile, Churchill also had another mission. Before leaving London for Cuba, Winston along with a friend, visited the British Army's Director of Military Intelligence, Colonel Edward Chapman (1840-1926), a veteran of Burmese and Afghan wars (the British Army won both wars). Winston wanted to know more about the situation in Cuba first. Colonel Chapman did a brief of the ongoing war in Cuba and provided maps for the young officers. There was information that a new kind of bullet was being used in the war. Chapman wanted to know more about it and Churchill's assignment in Cuba could help shed light on the power of this new bullet. He also instructed the two to gather information and statistics of everything war-related. In other words, Churchill's first military assignment was to be an amateur spy.

While Churchill's heart was with the Cuban rebels, he had to report and observe from the Spanish front. Secretly, he wanted the rebels to win because he observed how corrupt the Spaniards were. At the same time, he feared that if Spain won this war, more racial violence, corruption and revolt would follow.

Churchill's reports to the Daily Graphic perfectly captured these events. It was a week into his mission, during his 21st birthday, when Winston first heard bullets *"fired in anger,"* striking flesh or whistling through the air. He soon encountered more dangerous escapades, even witnessing violent deaths.

Back home, Churchill's escapades drew criticisms. A rival newspaper even questioned Winston's motive for going to Cuba, considering it wasn't a war where the British Empire was involved in. It further suggested that as a member of the Churchill family, Winston's decision to go to Cuba was extraordinary and that he should not fight other's battles. His friends meanwhile, hoped he would soon go home after witnessing the dangers of wars and decide to leave the army for good. They had anyway, been anticipating Winston's entrance to politics. They believed that he could do "remarkable things" as a politician.

Churchill's Cuban adventure eventually left an indelible mark in his life. There, he learned to smoke Havana cigars, which he continued until he died. He loved their quality and breadth. He also acquired the habit of long afternoon siestas, which enabled him to work long hours (until 3AM) until his old age. He also discovered the joy of drinking rum cocktails (unlike the American-style sugary kinds), which could've started his love for wine and many other alcoholic drinks (he wasn't a drunkard – though Hitler himself called Churchill once an "*insane drunkard*").

In the first week of December 1895, a week before returning to London, Churchill and fellow officer Barnes were recommended for Spain's military merit or award for gallantry, the Cross of Military Merit. In 1914, he also received a second award, the Cuban Campaign Medal, for his service in the Cuban war.

⚔ The Private University ⚔

The following year, after the mandatory seven months of training, Churchill saw himself leaving for Bangalore, south of India. He was still captivated by his days in Cuba. Reliving them, and despite the heat of Bangalore, Churchill started writing Savrola (published in 1900), a Ruritarian romance novel set in the Victorian era. It reflected his own political views during the Cuban War.

In secret, and although he knew it would eventually happen, Churchill dreaded the thought of going to India. In fact, he did everything to avoid his garrison duty in India. He took pains to talk to every connection his family had for any overseas military assignment, to no avail.

For Churchill, going to India was *"useless and unprofitable"*. He was too eager to make a name for himself at a young age that he believed going to India would delay to his ambitions. This he said to his mother in one of his letters, which he regularly wrote while stationed there until 1899. Lady Randolph suggested reading. This started Churchill's "private university."

Churchill started to read extensively. Even without her mother's urging however, he would still have done the same. At this point, because he saw no action in India, he became determined to pursue a career in politics. However, he did not have a degree in politics. He did not even go to a university. Self-education was his only answer.

To learn more about politics, Churchill religiously kept himself updated with political news from London. Aside from books about politics, history, and economics, he also read parliamentary debates. He even considered entering university, but was discouraged for his lack of knowledge in Greek and Latin, which were required for university entrance exams.

Historians however, have different views about Churchill's knowledge of the Latin language. Winston did know Latin, but wasn't enough for university standards. Back in his Harrow days, the school Headmaster, Reverend James Edward Cowell Welldon (1854-1937) already knew of this. However, Reverend Welldon gave the young Churchill a chance.

As it happened, the old headmaster was the Bishop of Calcutta by the time Winston was in India. Learning of his old Headmaster's illness at one time, Churchill went for a visit. Welldon, having known the young Churchill as a student, proclaimed that he expects the Lieutenant to be *"declaiming"* in the House of Commons soon. Churchill, on the other hand, did not deny or objected the thought.

⌇The Malakand Field Force ⌇

A year into his reading and writing, a conflict started to arise in India's Northwest Frontier. It was 1897.

Jack, Churchill's younger brother, believed that his older brother found contentment in danger. Prior to the Northwest conflict, Winston attempted to go to Greece and take action in the Greco-Turkish War. His plans were stopped when the war ended before he could get there. He had to look for his next adventure elsewhere.

Lieutenant Churchill in Bangalore, India in 1896. (c) Spectator UK

That same year, celebrations were arranged in London for Queen Victoria's Diamond Jubilee year. She had been on the throne for 60 years. While preparing to join the celebrations in London, Churchill heard news of a fight in India's Northwest Frontier, more than 2,000 miles away from Bangalore. Three British Army brigades had already been dispatched there. As expected and with the permission of his superior officer, Churchill joined the fight that was known as the First Mohmand Campaign (1897-1898). The Pashtun tribe (of Afghan origin) started a revolt against the British and Indians. They wanted total control of the Malakand Pass, a strategic point at the Peshawar border (between Afghanistan and Pakistan today) of the Northwest Frontier of British India.

British and Indian troops won the fight, but faced with hundreds of casualties. Churchill considered the fights in India more intense than he expected. He saw a fellow soldier hacked to death which prompted him to take revenge on the killer if not for his commanding officer's intervention.

In the end, Churchill was not sure whether his efforts for going there were worth it. Nonetheless, he acted capably and received the India Medal with the Punjab Frontier clasp after the campaign. He later published the whole ordeal in his first non-fiction book, The Story of the Malakand Field Force published the following year. His first published book was successful, gaining wide attention. This launched his career as an author.

While experiencing the war against the Punjab tribe, Churchill also wrote as a war correspondent for two newspapers – the Daily Telegraph (London) and The Pioneer (Allahabad, a city in Uttar Pradesh, north of India).

⚔ The Battle of Omdurman ⚔

After the war in India, Churchill went home to England. Upon hearing of his return, Prime Minister Lord Salisbury (officially Robert Arthur Talbot Gascoyne-Cecil, 3rd Marquess of Salisbury) called for him. Lord Salisbury had read Churchill's work, The Story of the Malakand Field Force, and was impressed with it. He offered the young officer any assistance that he may request, as a result. Without hesitation and with a hint of desperation, Churchill requested to be assigned in Egypt, as far away from India as possible. He didn't want to go back there.

In Sudan, there was another revolt, but this time by the Mahdists, against the Egyptian rule in Sudan. While looking forward to fighting another rebellion, Churchill was surprised to face a different kind of war – machine guns were in use. Winston himself declined to use his sword because of an old shoulder injury, but instead used his automatic Mauser pistol. When he was still at Sandhurst, he was in an accident while playing Polo which left him with a lifelong discomfort on his shoulder.

Granted permission, Churchill left for Cairo and was eventually assigned to the 21st Empress of India's Lancers (formed in 1759), still a Lieutenant and a war correspondent (for the Morning Post this time). On September 1898, a month after his arrival, Winston was assigned into the frontline in the city of Omdurman, Khartoum state, Sudan. Under the command of General Herbert Kitchener (1850-1916), the 21st Lancers were to clear the way onto Omdurman.

Charging, the 21st Lancers (only 400 of them) ran into a trap. First they thought there were only a few hundred enemies. They found out later there was actually two thousand troops hiding. It was one of the most dangerous situations Churchill got himself into. He later described the experience in his book, The River War, published in 1899.

After his service in the Sudan war, Churchill received the Queen's Sudan Medal and the Khedive's Sudan Medal with a Khartoum clasp.

⤜ First Oldham Election ⤛

Even before the war in Sudan ended, Churchill was already convinced to resign his commission as Lieutenant. He was more greatly interested in politics. Effective May 1899, Churchill resigned from the army.

Leaflet for Churchill's first election for the Oldham MP seat seen here with running mate, Mawdsley. (c) The British Museum via BBC UK

In a letter to his grandmother, the Duchess of Marlborough, Lady Frances Vane (1822-1899), Churchill explained his reason for leaving the army. To him, a career as a writer, war correspondent, or journalist, would provide more opportunities for what he considered as the *"larger ends of life."*

Soon, Winston was being courted by members of the Conservative party. They wanted him as their next candidate for the upcoming general election. This was what Churchill wanted; the "larger ends of life" as he knew was politics.

Robert Ascroft (in office 1895-1899), Member of Parliament (MP) for Oldham (in Manchester, England), invited Churchill to stand with him for the next general election. His running mate, another MP, James Oswald, was in bad health and couldn't run for another term. Churchill was more than willing to stand with Ascroft.

In an odd turn of events, Ascroft died before the election. Oswald on the other hand, resigned. Oldham became a constituency without MPs. A double by-election (to fill a vacant position in the middle of a term of office) was arranged to take place. Churchill took the stand with James Mawdsley, a client of Ascroft who was a lawyer.

The Conservative party believed Mawdsley would be a good candidate and match for Churchill because he was a trade union leader. He was also the General Secretary of the Amalgamated Association of Cotton Spinners for Lancashire. Back then, Oldham was a working class town. Having a trade union run for election would've been a sure win considering their rivals from the Liberal party, Alfred Emmot and Walter Runciman, were both from the rich class and owned huge companies. The Conservative party called the duo, their candidates, "The Scion and the Socialist."

Unfortunately, the match didn't work. Both lost the election. Battered, Churchill took solace in finding another adventure. He saw one in Africa.

✍ The Second Boer War ✍

Churchill's next destination was Ladysmith, a town in British South Africa. It was dominated by Boers, descendants of Dutch settlers who used to live in the area during the past century. Boer was the Afrikaans or Dutch word for farmer. Fearing occupation by the British Empire, Boers declared war against Britain.

Commissioned to write about the conflict for the Morning Post, Churchill sailed for South Africa on October 1899 just two days after the war broke out. He was able to close a monthly salary of $250 for this assignment, a considerable amount, making him the highest paid war correspondent of his time.

A group of war correspondents in South Africa during the Boer War. Churchill is seated second to the left, 1900. (c) Hulton Archive/Getty Images via Huffington Post UK

As a precaution for this assignment, Churchill kept himself armed throughout the journey with his trusty Mauser. When he arrived, he bumped into an old friend from India, Captain Aylmer Haldane (1862-1950) who was at that time, tasked to observe Boer territory through a railway towards the town of Ladysmith. Churchill joined them and offered his services to the captain should anything happen.

In the middle of the scouting expedition, their armored train came under fire from the Boers. Constant machine gun and artillery fire derailed several railcars, preventing the train from quickly retreating to safety. Churchill helped load the wounded onto a safe railcar then accompanied them to nearby Frere Station.

Churchill walked back to the scene of action to help the others who remained (Capt. Haldane included), but saw Boer soldiers capturing them. He jumped into a ditch to hide, but was still captured. Unfortunately, he left his Mauser pistol in the train's engine. Thankfully, the soldier who captured him did not shoot. Later in life, Louis Botha (1862-1919), the soldier who captured him eventually became the first Prime Minister of the Union of South Africa. He became friends with Churchill and even worked with him to help make South Africa a Dominion of the British Empire.

As a prisoner of war, Churchill was taken to Pretoria where he spent his 25th birthday behind bars. Back home, news of Churchill's efforts to rescue the train and his succeeding capture were reported by his fellow correspondents. He convinced the Boers that he was a civilian and that he shouldn't be taken as a prisoner, but they didn't listen. He even sent a letter to the Boer Secretary of State of War, but was also declined. They all read the news, unfortunately.

Haldane later convinced Churchill and Sergeant Major A. Brockie (of the Imperial Light Horse) to escape with him. While Churchill successfully scaled the wall, his two other fellow escapees were not. News of his escape once again reached home. The Boers on the other hand, put a price (£25) on his head, dead or alive.

Churchill meanwhile, jumped on a goods train and hid himself among sacks. Fortunately, he was not recognized in Pretoria. He went unnoticed until he ran across a goods train to Witbank and hopped on it. There, he was still miles away from Portuguese-occupied Mozambique, his destination.

Again, he was fortunate enough to come across the house of a British coal mine manager in Witbank. John Howard helped him hide in the mines. Once there, he asked the help of a British engineer, Dan Dewsnap, to lower

Churchill in the mines. Coincidentally, Dewsnap was from Oldham. Howard on the other hand, asked the assistance of Charles Burnham, a local storekeeper, to arrange Churchill's transfer. Burnham was to hide Churchill in cotton bales that were to be shipped in Portuguese East Africa.

Churchill's escape made him an overnight, national hero. His fellow local and international correspondents also took into writing his adventures. This made him an overnight, global sensation. Many believed, including his closest friends, that this would encourage him to go back to London.

However, instead of returning home, he chose to stay behind. He was commissioned by General Redvers Henry Buller (1839-1908) in a cavalry regiment, the South African Light Horse, under Major Julienne Byng (who later became Governor General of Canada in 1921-1926). He participated in six more battles in the next six months and joined General Ian Hamilton's (1853-1947) forces. He also went back to Pretoria to save his friends who were left captured by the Boers from the ambushed train.

After his service, Churchill received the Queen's South Africa Medal with six clasps. In July 1900, Churchill finally went home.

Churchill arrived home with manuscripts of his books about his war exploits. He published London to Ladysmith via Pretoria, an account of his capture in Pretoria, and the Ian Hamilton's March, his compiled experiences during the last six months he stayed in South Africa leading to the Relief of Ladysmith.

While his books were well-received, Churchill was widely-received as a military hero. He now has election experience and is ready to take Oldham again. This time, he won. Churchill's political career had just begun.

Chapter 3

✑LIFE IN POLITICS✑

I felt as though I were walking with destiny and that all my past life had been a preparation for this hour and for this trial.

-Winston Churchill, writing in his book The Second World War on becoming Prime Minister

$\mathscr{W}$inston Churchill returned to England in July 1900, a military hero. He used this opportunity to run for the Oldham MP seat again, still under the Conservative party. Thanks to his war and election experiences, Churchill won his first Parliamentary MP seat in 1900. He was only 26 years old.

✑The Campaign and the Khaki Election ✑

The 1900 general election was christened the Khaki Election for the recent British victory in the Boer War in South Africa. The South African Light Horse regiment, of which Churchill became a member, used to have a Khaki-colored uniform.

From the start, it was evident for the Conservative party that Churchill could win the Oldham MP seat because of his prior experience in South Africa where the Boer War took place. They made sure that their candidate would exploit his war adventures to the fullest.

In one of Churchill's public addresses, he further increased the patriotic mood of the voting people by asking them to support and continue the work and achievements of the noble soldiers who served in South Africa by voting for him, and by doing so, they can proclaim to other European nations that England will do its best to preserve its Empire and set an example to others.

Remembering South Africa, Churchill fought in the Boer War and six other battles that ensued. An Oldham native, Dan Dewsnap, helped him hide from the Boers during his escape. Dewsnap prophetically told Churchill that if he ever runs as MP for Oldham, "They'll all vote for you next time."

Churchill did win and proved Dewsnap right. Upon his return to Oldham after the war, he was practically welcomed by massed crowds and accompanying brass brands. He gave a speech in the local Theater Royal in which he mentioned Dewsnap to which the crowd roared, collectively beaming.

As early as April 1900, the Southport Conservative Association has approached Churchill to run as their candidate. However, his heart was with the Oldham people. According to him, the Oldham people have convinced him not to desert them.

For the Khaki Election, Churchill stood with Charles Chrisp as his running mate. The previous one, James Mawdsley, has already retired from the political scene due to a freak accident where the porcelain bathtub he was bathing in broke because of his heavy weight. The old man received life-threatening injuries as a result.

Churchill took his campaign seriously, even convincing his mother to help him. Lady Randolph anyways, was famous in London that time. What compelled him however, to ask for his mother's help was that he was still unmarried. Many of his counterparts, and even his running mate, had a wife campaigning for their own husbands. Reluctantly, Lady Randolph went to Oldham to help his son, but not without complaining for the lack of accommodations in the working class town for a woman like her.

Another prominent figure helped Churchill in his campaigns. For the most part of his political career, he had always been in constant disagreement with the Chamberlains. However and surprisingly, during his early venture in politics, one of the most famous Conservative politicians, Joseph Chamberlain (1836-1914), then Secretary of State for the Colonies, helped him. In fact, it was Chamberlain who ensured that the topic of the Boer War be the focal point of that year's election.

On October 1, 1900, the Oldham result was declared. Churchill won an MP seat, though the Liberals maintained majority of the seats in the House of Commons.

Lord Salisbury, former Prime Minister and fan of Churchill's war books, wrote to congratulate the newly elected MP. He believed that Churchill's adventures in South Africa had cemented his place in the minds of Oldham voters who had always been a difficult town to persuade in voting for Conservative candidates.

✒ The Conservative Churchill ✒

Churchill took pleasure in his infant career as a politician. However, the Oldham constituency was quick to criticize his rule and leadership. He was a remote figure in their midst; distant in truth.

Churchill at his desk after winning Oldham MP 1900. (c) Rischgitz and Stringer via BBC UK

Churchill returned to writing and lecturing about his war adventures after becoming an MP. He stopped doing the two after the war in South Africa. He wanted to focus on his campaign for Oldham MP. He toured Great Britain to provide lectures. He also left for the United States and Canada for the same reason. Throughout his trips, he wrote the Lord Randolph Churchill, a critically-acclaimed two-volume biography of his late father. On January 1901, upon hearing news of Queen Victoria's death, he returned to London.

At Oldham, he did involve himself in some local, common requests for money and support from local institutions. He was also requested to patronize local tax collector, sanitary inspectors, and various local businesses.

In the House of Commons in London, Churchill delivered his first speech on February 1901. The house was full. He started by proclaiming that the Boers in South Africa should have a civil government instead of a military government which its British rulers wish to impose. By the end of his speech, he mentioned his father who once stood where he was, delivering his own speech.

As Oldham MP, Churchill was not shy when opposing his party leaders. From Army Reform to the dismissal of an allegedly-erring officer, Churchill opposed them all, even gaining the support of some Liberals. At one point, he joined forces with other young Conservative MPs, led by Lord Hugh Cecil (1869-1956), to annoy their own party leaders. They were called the "Hughligans."

The main event during Churchill's time as Oldham MP however, was his fallout with the Conservative Party which led him to resign his seat.

There was a debate about whether taxes should be imposed on imported goods and foods. It caused a rift within the Conservative Party. One wing, led by Joseph Chamberlain, wanted to introduce taxes, while the other wing, to which Churchill sided, promoted Free Trade. This went on for a few years until in May 1903, when Churchill disagreed again with a new tax reform that Chamberlain was faithfully defending. He stood his ground and went against the influential Chamberlain. He resigned from his Oldham MP seat and sided with the Liberals. Again, he stood by his belief in the Victorian policy of Free Trade.

Historians were puzzled of Churchill's embrace of the Free Trade policy. He was not expected to go against what majority of the Conservative Party wanted to impose, let alone disagree with Chamberlain, the man who helped him win. However, it could either be his principles were aligned with Free Trade, or that he wanted to create noise again, so that he could be noticed within the House of Commons.

Unfortunately, Churchill's move to promote Free Trade was not well-received by the Oldham constituency and many other conservative clubs. The Marlborough Conservative Club for one, declared their protest for Churchill's "hostile attitude" towards the new tax reforms. In another, the North Chadderton Conservative Club, Churchill was physically prevented from speaking in their meeting. Back at his constituency, the Oldham Conservative Association in October 1903 suggested to Churchill that he should find his platform on the side of the Liberal Party.

The violent reactions reached its height when on December 1903, a motion of no-confidence in Churchill was passed by the General Purposes Committee of the Oldham Conservative Party. A month after the motion, it was decided that Churchill was no longer the official Conservative representative for the town of Oldham.

Churchill could've resigned. Considerable negotiations however, decided that the move wouldn't benefit both parties. As a result, Churchill stayed as MP for Oldham until the next general election in 1906.

◢ The Liberal Churchill ◣

It was Churchill's belief that by coming up with the tax reforms, the Conservatives had forgotten and neglected their principles. Because of this, he attacked his old party ferociously, especially Chamberlain. He wasn't alone in his actions. Along with David Lloyd George (1863-1945) and John Morley (1838-1923), both MPs from the Liberal Party and surprisingly were against the Boer War, Churchill became bolder of his criticisms against Chamberlain.

At the end of May 1904, Churchill finalized his move to the Liberal Party. He crossed the floor of the House of Commons and took up a seat on the benches of the Liberal opposition. Four years into the Parliament, he was now a Liberal.

Churchill giving a speech in by-election campaign in North West Manchester, 1908. (c) Daily Herald Archives via Daily Mail UK

Meanwhile, while his political career was taking a new turn, Churchill's private life also did a turn, though unnoticed. It was in 1904 when Churchill first met Clementine Hozier, his future wife, who was making her social debut. Robert Offley Ashburton Crewe-Milnes (1858-1945), Earl of Crewe, held a summer ball in their town residence, the Crewe House, with 29-year old Churchill in attendance (with his Private Secretary and lifelong friend, Sir Edward Marsh (1872-1953). Unfortunately, Winston was too confused with another love interest, that his meeting with Clementine went fruitless.

Focusing on his political career, Churchill was selected by his new party to stand as MP candidate a few days later after crossing the floor. The Liberals wanted him to run for Northwest Manchester MP in the coming general election in 1906. Apparently, his opposed views of the tax reforms paid off. He grew such noise that he won the 1906 election. From being an MP for Northwest Manchester, Churchill's political career rose rapidly. He was assigned as Undersecretary for the Colonies, in which he defended South Africa's policy of self-government and gained credit for it.

Aside from his local duties, Churchill continued to travel extensively. He was frequently invited to witness maneuver training in other European countries including Germany and France. He also visited South Africa again and other African countries. While abroad, the press followed his journey. He was always in the newspapers. He also regularly wrote to his mother, brother, and the Colonial office he was serving in. At the same time, he was given permission to send reports of his trips to King Edward VII, Queen Victoria's successor.

In 1908, King Edward VII, along with Herbert Henry Asquith (officially 1st Earl of Oxford and Asquith), then Chancellor of the Exchequer, heard rumors that Churchill wanted to become a minister. Soon, everybody in the House of Commons anticipated Churchill's new appointment. In March, while also anticipating his succession as Prime Minister following Sir Henry Campbell-Bannerman's (in office 1905-1908) resignation due to failing health, Asquith offered Churchill three options as soon as Campbell-Bannerman steps down. He could either choose an appointment in the Admiralty, Local Government Board, or the Colonial Office. Churchill chose the latter. He wanted to keep his post as undersecretary and made his intentions clear. However, the King had something else in his mind and so, when Asquith seated as a Liberal PM (in office 1908-1916), he assigned Churchill into the Board of Trade as its President.

Meanwhile, and yet again, Churchill's private life took another fateful turn. In the spring of 1908, on the night of his Cabinet appointment, he met Clementine again, this time in a dinner party hosted by the Baroness of St. Helier, Susan Elizabeth Mary Jeune (1845-1931). Churchill and Clementine sat beside each other, although neither wanted to be there in the first place. He apparently made a bad impression on her which at the end, became the opposite. Clementine later described that Churchill's "charm and brilliancy" won her over.

The following months, Churchill was to court Clementine although she was away in Europe, accompanying her mother in the trip. They constantly wrote each other. When she returned, they always took advantage of social gatherings to see each other. It was unacceptable back then for single women to dine or lunch alone with men, married or not.

Winston on the other hand, as Board Trade President, together with Earl Lloyd-George, he pioneered social reforms that forever changed the welfare state. They created a program that featured unemployment insurance, labor exchanges, laws on sweated labor (imposing 8-hour work days), fixed minimum wages, and old-age pensions.

In private life, Churchill was finally settling down. In August of the same year, Churchill proposed to Clementine at the Temple of Diana (they later named their firstborn, Diana) in the gardens of the Blenheim Palace. His brother Jack meanwhile, got married. The following September, Churchill married Clementine at St. Margaret's Church in Westminster Abbey, officiated by Bishop of St. Asaph, Alfred George Edwards and with Lord Hugh Cecil ("leader" of the "Hughligans") as the Best Man. King Edward was not able to attend, but did sent a congratulatory note. In the summer of the following year in 1909, Diana was born.

Winston with fiancée Clementine shortly before their marriage, 1908. (c) Wikipedia

On the political front, Churchill continued to fight for his belief in Free Trade. As President of Board Trade, he blocked the budget proposal of Reginald McKenna (though also a Liberal), First Lord of the Admiralty (in office 1908-1911), for acquisition of Navy dreadnaught warships. He, together with Chancellor of the Exchequer David George (in office 1908-1915), wanted the funds to go to the People's Budget, which meant increasing taxes on the wealthy and distributing them for social welfare programs. It is a first in British history that the money of the wealthy be distributed to the general public. For this, Churchill and George were called by the Conservatives as the "terrible twins."

Although the bill for the People's Budget was vigorously campaigned by Churchill and his Budget League, which he was a president, it was disallowed by the House of Lords (majority was Conservatives), or the upper house of the Parliament. However, after the general election of 1910, the Liberals gained majority of the seats in the Lords, reducing their power. As a result, the People's Budget was passed in April. It was another victory for Churchill.

Within two years since he became a cabinet minister, he was to become the Home Secretary. Back then, it was only him and Sir Robert Peel (1788-1850) in 1866 who were the youngest ones to hold the position at the age of 36.

Churchill introduced prison reforms as Home Secretary, which made petty crimes punishable with a few days jail time only. Capital punishments should only be reserved for serious, heinous crimes. However, the growing social unrest and labor strikes dominated Churchill's mind. He was after all, in charge of law and order as Home Secretary. The events that ensued led to the infamous Tonypandy Riots were troops were sent in (as requested by the chief constable to the War Office) by Churchill to help police disperse the rioters. Unfortunately, many were not happy with his decision. To this day, views about Churchill's involvement in the riot are divided.

Churchill's political career was thriving. As Secretary of State for the Home Office, he maintained a nightly report of House proceedings to the new King, George V. King Edward VII has died in May 1910. The following June, George V became the ruling monarch.

⚔ As First Lord of the Admiralty ⚔

In May 1911, Churchill's second child, Randolph, was born. A few months later, PM Asquith appointed Churchill to the Committee on Imperial Defence. It was during this time that he first saw the aggressiveness of Germany's troops. While in Morocco with Lloyd George, they witnessed a German gunboat intimidating the French (because they had claims on the Moroccan port). In case a war ensues, Churchill believed that England should side with France.

In the same year, Churchill was assigned the post as First Lord of the Admiralty. By the time he assumed office, he was more than convinced that Germany was planning to go to war and wanted to control Europe. Because of this, he wanted the Royal Navy to be prepared for what might happen next. First, he reorganized the navy's high command and then toured (together with PM Asquith) to the Mediterranean to check on the British Fleet. He further campaigned for the expansion and modernization of the Royal Navy, all along embarking on most of the ships and spending months there.

Churchill inspecting the boys from a training ship, 1912. (c) Hulton Archive/Getty Images via Huffington Post UK

However, Churchill once again drew enemies because of his decisions. From changing the leadership (Sea Lords) in the navy, to naming the ships and spending time there, there were always heavy criticisms. What annoyed his enemies more was his budget proposal for the modernization and expansion of the navy. To this, his ally and friend George, criticized him. In the end, Churchill achieved success.

Chapter 4

☙ WORLD WAR I AND AFTER ☙

We shall fight on the beaches, we shall fight on the landing grounds, we shall fight on the fields... we shall never surrender.

-Winston Churchill, June 1940

$\mathcal{G}$ermany wanted Austria to reconcile with Greece, Serbia, and Romania. Austria however, wanted to align with Turkey and Bulgaria instead. Heir to the throne in Austria, Archduke Franz Ferdinand and wife Sophie were touring in Sarajevo, in support of loyal Slav nationalist when they were assassinated by Serbians. It was June 1914. Europe, as Churchill expected, was at the brink of war. A month later, Germany declared war on Russia and in August, they invaded Belgium.

While Churchill saw it personally to organize defense for Belgium, his third child, Sarah, was born in October 1914.

Again, many were in disagreement with his decision regarding Belgium because many men died. However, his defense became a success when the Belgian army was able to escape from the Germans. The French ports of Dunkirk and Calais in turn, were saved.

However, a miscalculated move during the Dardanelles (also Gallipoli) Campaign (1915) in Turkey caused Churchill his position. The world viewed the Allies (British, French,

Australian, New Zealand, and Indian troops) lacked in military leadership, experience, strategies, and equipment because of the operation. PM Asquith, together with the Unionists, decided to form a new National Government. This would leave his good friend without a position even though he was the Lord of Admiralty. As a result of Asquith's decision, Churchill resigned from office. Asquith followed. The succeeding PM became Churchill's previous ally, David Lloyd George.

After his resignation, Churchill was appointed as Chancellor of the Duchy of Lancaster, though he was again offered a top role in the Colonial Office. He now had a lower salary, diminished power, and was without a residence since he had to vacate Whitehall, the Admiralty House. According to the official biographer of Churchill, Sir Martin Gilbert (1936-2015), this was one of the lowest points in the life of Winston. To this, Mrs. Churchill agrees because she did feel the same way. According to her, the Dardanelles operation haunted Churchill for the rest of his life.

In the Churchill household, the gloom was evident. How could it not be when they are to be moved to a temporary housing? They lived in the Admiralty House since Churchill took office and now they had to live with relatives. They eventually rented their own place in Surrey. It was during this time that Winston learned of a hobby he used as a therapy for years to come. Goonie (Lady Gwendolin Bertie 1885–1941, daughter of the 7th Earl of Abingdon), as the Churchills fondly called Jack's (Churchill's brother) wife, was painting one day when she noticed how intently Winston was looking at what she was doing. She convinced him to try it out and it was the start of Churchill's lifelong hobby of painting whenever he was feeling down.

As Chancellor, Churchill was tasked to go to Dardanelles and report back to PM Asquith. However, the plan did not push through, to Churchill's disappointment. For this, he asked permission from Asquith if he could resign, to which the PM granted.

Churchill wanted to go to France and join the army fighting. He trained in trench combat before leaving for France. In January 1916, he was appointed to command an infantry battalion as Lieutenant Colonel of the 6th Royal Scots Fusiliers. However, six months later, he returned to Parliament (now under the coalition government of PM Lloyd George) and opted to become a private member.

A year later in March 1917, after the publication of the Dardanelles report, it was revealed that Churchill was not to blame for the disaster that happened. Four months later, he was officially back in the government as Minister of Munitions. By November 1918, the First World War was over. Four days later, the Churchills' fourth child, Marigold, was born

✍ After World War I 1919-1929 ✍

Two years later in 1919, Churchill became Secretary of War. During this time, he made sure to let everybody know that Germany is a constant threat to the Allies and Europe. He also focused on the Irish Free State, Bolsheviks in Russia, and the Kurdish war in Iraq. He also oversaw the signing of alliance treaty between France, the U.S., and Britain.

Despite being constantly busy, Churchill still had ample time for his family. In the summer of 1922, he bought the Chartwell Manor, a farm estate in Westerham, Kent, England. It was perfect for his growing family now that finally, his fifth and last child, Mary, was born.

The same year, Churchill's friend, PM Lloyd George resigned, succeeded by Andrew Bonar Law (in office 1922-1923), a Conservative. The coalition government formed by George, Law, and Asquith was dissolved. A general election had to be put into place. During this time, Churchill was not well enough to campaign for himself because of undergoing an appendectomy (removal of appendix following a rupture). As a result, he lost his position. He was known to have said, *"Without an office, without a seat, without a party, and without an appendix."*

Without a seat in the new government, Churchill spent his time writing about the war. The first volume of his war journals, The World Crisis, received both praises and criticisms. It was published in April 1923.

The public started to speculate about Churchill's future in the political scene after reading his book. While his friends from the previous governments also had their own political crises, they still had seats in the new Parliament. He did not. He was angry at PM Law for breaking the coalition government, but still creating the same mistakes in his current administration.

Meanwhile, in the Churchill household, summer was to be spent in Sussex Square. Chartwell Manor was being renovated. Winston on the other hand, started the second volume of The World Crisis. He also took a well-deserved and much awaited vacation in the Mediterranean with the Duke of Westminster, William Grosvenor (1894–1963).

Churchill's close friends always encouraged him to reenter politics again. From 1923 to 1924, he ran in two by-elections: West Leicester (December 1923) and Westminster (March 1924). He was defeated in both. However, his Westminster campaign was his last for the Liberal Party. He was eyeing the Conservatives again. He believed he was always a Conservative. In May 1924, he delivered his first speech in a Conservative meeting, the first in twenty years since he became a Liberal. This was the second time Churchill had crossed the floor, although he was without an official seat at that time. He was now a Conservative again.

Through the following months, Churchill continued his public speaking engagements. When summer arrived, the constituency of Epping (Essex, England), with the initiative of the town's Conservative Party's Constituency Committee, invited Winston to run as a "Constitutionalist" considering he didn't want to be associated with PM Baldwin's Labour Government. He believed that the British Constitution was not being fully supported by Baldwin's government.

In October 1924, Churchill finally won a seat. However, he was in for a surprise when Baldwin offered him the second-highest position in the Parliament, the Chancellor of Exchequer. Of course, Churchill accepted, but not without criticism from the Conservative Party.

At first, Churchill's handle of the office was doing well. However, his reintroduction of the Gold Standard was a disaster. It caused deflation and many lost their jobs, eventually leading to the Great Strike of 1926. This led to the defeat of the Conservative government in the general election of 1929. Since then, Churchill experienced distrust. He was thought of as reckless, lacking stability and judgment. By the time the new National Government was formed in 1931, he was not invited to take part. This started Churchill's "wilderness years."

✦ Wilderness Years 1930-1939 ✦

Winston spent his time writing, speaking in lectures, and painting, all as usual. However, it was during this time that he received vital information about the situation in Germany. Through Major Desmond Morton (1891-1971), a neighbor in Chartwell, Churchill was able to learn about the increasing power of Nazi Germany's military. He did not waste time to convince the government that Germany, sooner or later, will become a huge threat not only to Britain, but for the whole Europe. It was like going back to World War I again.

At the Chartwell Mansion, with the help of Professor Frederick Lindemann (1st Viscount Cherwell 1886-1957), he built an intelligence center that was considered better and superior that what the government currently had. Here, he gathered enough intelligence of the impending threat that Germany was posing. The government brushed his gathered intelligence aside, paying no attention.

A few years into his political isolation, Churchill was considered several times for a position in the Cabinet, mostly concerning positions related to war. However, proposals for his return were always met with resistance. Baldwin never again gave Churchill a seat in the House while he was Prime Minister. Although Churchill did receive a special membership into Baldwin's air-research defense, a secret committee for gathering intelligence. On the other hand, his friends encouraged him to make his voice heard, especially about Hitler.

During the Wilderness Years, Churchill also campaigned against the independence of India. He was even critical of Mahatma Gandhi's (1869-1948) disobedience revolt and choice of clothing. He wanted British power to remain in India. Also during the wilderness years, Churchill witnessed the death of King George V (1936), abdication of King Edward VIII (1936), and the coronation of his successor, King George VI (1937).

Neville Chamberlain (half-brother to Austen Chamberlain, one of Churchill's closest friends, and son to Joseph Chamberlain, Churchill's former senior in the Conservative party) succeeded Baldwin as Prime Minister in 1937. Churchill persisted on his stance about Germany, but was still ignored until sudden events confirmed his warnings. However, Neville was keen on appeasing Hitler as the Nazis began to control its neighbors. First it was Austria. In the

Munich Agreement of 1938, Neville (along with Italy and France) sacrificed Czechoslovakia (through Sudetenland, a German-speaking region) to Germany. Churchill was receiving a growing number of sympathizers (and believers) during this time and by early 1939, the majority wanted him back in the government. Neville however, stood his ground.

On September 1, 1939, Hitler invaded Poland. UK in turn, declared war on Germany. Churchill was immediately called for office. His political exile, the Wilderness Years, was now over. World War II has just begun.

Chapter 5

⚔WORLD WAR II AND AFTER⚔

You were given the choice between war and dishonour. You chose dishonour and you will have war.

-Winston Churchill, reaction to Neville Chamberlain's move to sign an agreement with Germany in 1938

"Winston is back."

𝒫M Chamberlain sent a message to the British fleet after he appointed Churchill member of the War Cabinet and as the First Lord of the Admiralty, a post Winston once held in 1911. It was three days since Hitler invaded Poland and that day, September 3, at 11AM, Britain was to declare war against Germany.

In the U.S., then President Franklin D. Roosevelt heard of the news. They were not yet involved in the war, but he did send a congratulatory note to Churchill for returning from his political exile and for his new post in the British government. Their constant, fateful correspondence early in the war began.

For the first nine months of the Second World War, the absence of land operations from both the Allies and the Germans led to the Phony Wars. The only action that was evident to the rest of Europe during this time was Soviet Union's naval attack on Finland.

Back at home, and despite being back in the Parliament, Churchill was still met with hostilities. As the First Lord of the Admiralty, he first wanted Britain to occupy the neutral port of Norway and Sweden as a strategic precautionary measure, but Chamberlain's government didn't allow him to. As a result, the operation was delayed and Germany eventually invaded Norway.

✂ German Supply Lines ✂

It was April 1940 and Churchill has just been assigned the chairmanship of the Military Coordinating Committee. He also wanted to float mines in the river Rhine to cripple German supply lines, but the French were afraid that it would provoke Germany to invade them if Churchill's propose would be done. To persuade the French, Winston left for Paris only to be unsuccessful of his endeavor.

Meanwhile in Germany, Hitler was already organizing invasion of the Scandinavian country. Churchill had intelligence information of this and proposed the pre-emptive occupation of Norway, an important route for the German army. Iron ore was mined from Kiruna in Sweden and transported through the port of Narvik in Norway.

After the invasion of Narvik, Churchill was not discouraged. He believed that there was still something that could make things right. His supporters advocated action in Norway, but were not sure which other ports to occupy. Trondheim, south of Norvik, was to be targeted. However, those plans did not push through or were not approved by Chamberlain's government. In Norway, Hitler was discreetly sending and landing paratroopers. Eventually, it fell to the Nazis.

The occupation of Norway was a setback for Neville. He resisted Churchill's proposal to prevent aggression by the Germans and the only way this was possible was to independently occupy important Norwegian iron mines and sea ports. The failure of the Narvik, Trondheim, and Kiruna expeditions, which were dependent on naval support, called to mind the disaster that happened during the Dardanelles Campaign in World War I where Churchill was blamed. This time however, it was Chamberlain. Surprisingly, it was Churchill who campaigned to defend him. While all this was happening, Britain and her allies were losing the war.

⚔ Prime Minister Sir Winston Churchill ⚔

On 7 May 1940, debate on the war effort began in the Parliament. Speakers on both Liberal and Conservative sides of the House criticized and reprimanded the Government for its lack of will and its failures to prevent Germany from moving forward. The Norwegian disaster, of course, was also discussed. A voting was made which led to a vote of no confidence against PM Chamberlain.

Silently again, Hitler was creeping towards the Low Countries. Three days after the Parliamentary debate in Britain, Germany marched down towards Netherlands, Belgium and Luxembourg. As this happened, Chamberlain was pressured to resign, which he did. He wanted the Secretary of State for Foreign Affairs Lord Halifax (Edward Frederick Lindley Wood, 1st Earl of Halifax 1881-1959), to succeed him, but Halifax wisely declined.

Churchill was seen as the only alternative leader with distinguished credibility considering his war experience and knowledge. While the current Labor Party didn't trust Churchill and viewed him as anti-Socialist, they also recognized his unwavering commitment to defeat Hitler.

Churchill on his desk as Prime Minister, 1940. (c) Wikipedia

Just within a few hours of Chamberlain's resignation, the Nazis began its Western Offensive. The German Blitzkrieg was being unleashed. They invaded the Netherlands, Belgium and Luxembourg. King George VI immediately appointed Churchill as prime minister and minister of defense.

Traditionally, a prime minister could not advise a ruling monarch to choose a successor for the outgoing post. However, Chamberlain wanted the major parties in the House of Commons (Conservative, Labor, and Liberal parties) to support the next prime minister. Thus, a meeting between Chamberlain, David Margesson (Government Chief Whip, in office 1931-1940), and Churchill went underway. The meeting led to the recommendation of Winston as the next prime minister. King George VI, as the constitutional monarch, then asked Churchill for the post.

Churchill took serious responsibility for the war effort. He was credited with boosting morale for the British people during periods of overwhelming hardships. Also, most of his memorable speeches were given during World War II.

Two days later after Churchill sat as Prime Minister, the Nazis attacked France. Without the Scandinavian and Low Countries, Britain stood alone against the blitz.

✄ The German Blitzkrieg ✄

The coalition government that was eventually formed under Churchill strengthened the War Cabinet with five powerful players. It included former PM Chamberlain, Lord Halifax, Arthur Greenwood and Clement Attlee. The latter two were leaders of the Labor Party. The cabinet became a powerful agency as it included representative of all major parties in the House of Commons. It made swift decisions considering its influence within each of its own parties. It made sure that all voices were heard and proposals were well-represented.

On May 13 Churchill delivered his first speech in the House of Commons as the new Prime Minister. Here, he uttered one of his famous words:

"I have nothing to offer but blood, toil, tears and sweat."

Within a couple of weeks, the Parliament gave emergency powers to the PM Churchill. It passed legislation requiring all people from the UK and the British Empire their services and property to be used by the Crown for the victory of the war. To date, it's one of the most far-reaching emergency powers ever granted in modern British history.

At first, the burden of supervising the withdrawal of troops from the beaches of Dunkirk (Battle of Dunkirk in France) fell in the hands of Churchill. Fortunately, General Harold Alexander supervised the withdrawal of more than 330,000 men there, saving them from sure death. After the defeat and evacuation of British forces, Churchill warned Parliament that there is a real risk of invasion now that France has collapsed. He made repeated visits to the France to convince the French government to remain in the war fighting. This led to the Anglo-French union on June 16, 1940.

However, many French leaders did not want the agreement. To them, they would rather be a Nazi province than become part of the British Dominion (or colony), which was apart from what Churchill was aiming. He didn't want the French Navy to end up in the hands of the Nazis, something that the Germans would find advantageous.

When all this failed, Paris fell in the hands of Nazis on June 14, 1940. Hitler himself went to France to accept their surrender. The following decision to be made caused Churchill nothing but anguish.

Over growing concerns with France's relationship with the Germans, Churchill decided to destroy some of its fleet. Alternatives were given to the French with the aim of preventing them from handing their ships to the Germans. Some of the ships went to the British side voluntarily, while some were demilitarized. However, the French fleet in French-occupied Oran in Algeria had to be attacked by the Royal Navy. This way, when the fleet is to be surrendered to Hitler, it would not be intact any longer.

While Churchill was saddened by the force imposed on the French Fleet, he found support from the US President Roosevelt. Roosevelt, while they were not yet involved in the war, believed that Churchill should do his best in fighting for Britain and the Commonwealth.

Churchill made one of his most memorable speeches to the House of Commons on June 18, 1940 where he said:

"Let us therefore brace ourselves to our duty and so bear ourselves that if the British Empire and its Commonwealth lasts for a thousand years men will still say, 'This was their finest hour'."

During his speech, Churchill warned that the Battle of Britain was about to begin. On July 10, the first bombing raid began.

✺ The Battle of Britain ✺

Britain's first defense against the Luftwaffe, or the German Air Force bombers was the Fighter Command headed by Sir Hugh Dowding (Air Chief Marshal and 1st Baron Dowding 1882–1970). Sir Dowding's own son was one of the air fighters. Six days later, Hitler wanted a landing operation against England, with the code name Sea Lion, and issued an order for it.

The Battle of Britain greatly energised Churchill, who was 65 years old at the time. He did what he knew best. He went to the firing line, visited the fighter headquarters, and inspected coast defenses or antiaircraft batteries. He also visited bomb damage sites and victims of the blitz; all the while giving his V sign and smoking his cigar. He also delivered broadcasting reports to the British people with his usual dark Churchillian humor and rhetoric. The nation loved him.

On 14 August Roosevelt sent a message to Churchill offering aircraft and destroyers if he agreed to allow US naval and air bases on British colonies in North America. Churchill immediately accepted. He fervently believed that US assistance would bring him victory.

Meanwhile, the air war and bombing raid raged over Britain. On 20 August, Churchill gave another of his iconic anecdotes recognizing the contributions and sacrifices of the young soldiers who were challenging the German air force on a daily basis. Churchill commented,

"Never in the field of human conflict was so much owed by so many to so few."

Four days later, the Luftwaffe began bombing central London in broad daylight. A few weeks later, more than two hundred German bombers attacked London. Churchill visited the damaged streets the next day. Sir Dowding's detailed preparation and prudent management proved him successful in the assault. Likewise, the rest of the conquered people of Europe admired Churchill's leadership and saw him as a beacon of hope.

On 17 September, Hitler ceased his assault and postponed Operation Sea Lion.

ᴄ The Axis Powers ᴄ

However, the British victory in the Battle of Britain was not to be celebrated, yet. On September 27, ten days after Hitler postponed Sea Lion, a pact was signed between Italy (under Benito Mussolini), Japan (under Emperor Hirohito) and Germany. They were known as the Axis Powers. Minor members included Hungary, Bulgaria, and Romania.

In October, Churchill was made leader of the Conservative Party. This was considered a remarkable achievement since he left them and crossed the floor to the Liberals in 1904. Clementine, Churchill's wife, believed this was a mistake and made it evident to her husband.

Meanwhile, the bombing in England continued, especially at night. In retaliation, the British air fighters conducted bombing raids on various targets, including Berlin. Churchill was confident of victory. However, he believed this would only happen if the US became an ally.

ᴄ The Grand Alliance ᴄ

Soon enough, the alliance was set. On 17 December Roosevelt announced the Lend-Lease policy. It provided essential supplies to Britain on credit. As a result, Churchill was able to extend its arms to Soviet Union (under Joseph Stalin) as it was suddenly attacked by the Nazis.

Churchill was always against Communism. However, he believed that if Russia is in danger, Britain would be in danger as well. Eventually, he also pledged aid to the people of Russia.

In the events that followed, Churchill decided to form the grand alliance, including Soviet Union and the United States. However, it was not until 1942 when the Anglo-Soviet Pact of Mutual Assistance was signed. Eventually in 1945, the United Nations was formed on the basis of the Allied nations.

Churchill with Stalin (left) and Roosevelt (center) in Teheran Conference in Iran, 1943. (c) Huffington Post UK

⚔ World War II Ends ⚔

The US finally entered World War II after Japan attacked Pearl Harbor in December 1941. This made Churchill confident that the Allies would win the war. He was right. On September 2, 1945, after six years and 1 day of war, World War

II ended when the documents of surrender by Japan was signed both by the US and the Japanese.

On June 1944, D-Day (also Invasion of Normandy or Normandy Landings) was underway. The Allies invaded Normandy (France) and the German forces were defeated. Elsewhere in Europe, German forces were being pushed back by the Allies.

On December the same year, German forces made its last attempt of an offensive campaign in the Battle of the Bulge (in the Ardennes region). It lasted for more than one month, ending in January 1945. Allies continued to push towards Germany. By the end of April, the Reichstag was captured and Hitler committed suicide. Berlin surrendered on May 1945.

In Asia, the war raged with Japan on the offensive. They were losing the war, but reluctant to surrender even after the Allies called for one. As a result, the US decided to bomb Hiroshima and Nagasaki in early August. A few weeks later, Japan surrendered. The papers were signed on September 2 which ended the Second World War.

In the months leading to the Allied victory, Churchill worked closely with Roosevelt and Stalin to forge a war strategy against the Axis and to talk about post-world war policies. The Allies held meetings throughout the war in Teheran (1943), Yalta (February 1945) and Potsdam (July 1945 – Roosevelt died in April. He was replaced by President Harry Truman). It was during one of these meetings that the foundations for the United Nations were formed.

Back in Britain, as his social reforms failed to convince the public, the general election in July 1945 brought him defeat. However, Churchill continued to be the Leader of the Opposition. In 1946, he gave his famous "Iron Curtain" speech, warning the world of the domination of Eastern Europe by the Soviets.

In 1951, Churchill was elected into office again.

Chapter 6

✐ IN MEMORY ✐

Be of good cheer. The time of your deliverance will come. The soul of freedom is deathless; it cannot, and will not, perish.

-Winston Churchill, September 1940, in a broadcast during WWII

*B*ack in office as Prime Minister again, Churchill was also appointed again as Minister of Defense from October 1951 to January 1952. The following year, he was knighted by Queen Elizabeth II as Garter Knight (Order of the Garter). He was supposed to gain a peerage (noble, hereditary titles) to the rank of duke (as Duke of London), but he declined (to the dismay of his only son, Randolph).

For the next two years, Churchill introduced two important domestic reforms in Britain. He helped improve the working condition of miners through reforms. He eventually introduced the Mines and Quarries Act of 1954. In 1955 meanwhile, he helped establish standards for housing in the UK through his Housing Repairs and Rent Act.

However, a series of foreign policy crises overshadowed his domestic reforms. In the Kenya and Malaya colonies, Churchill ordered direct military action against the uprising rebellion. The military action proved to be successful in putting down the rebellions. However, it was from these incidents that it became clear that colonial rule can no longer be sustained by Britain.

On the other hand, Churchill's failing health prevented him from performing his duties as Prime Minister. He resigned in 1955 and was succeeded by Anthony Eden (husband of Churchill's niece, Clarissa Spencer Churchill).

Churchill leaving his London home in Hyde Park to go to the House of Commons, 1964. (c) Huffington Post UK

As early as 1941, Churchill had already been showing signs of fragile health. In 1943, he suffered from pneumonia and even had a mild heart attack. In June 1953, he had a series of strokes while in his office. News of it however, was kept from the Parliament and the public. His absence was announced only to declare that he has suffered from exhaustion and that he needed rest. He took a few months rest at home and resumed his job as Prime Minister in October. However, it became obvious that he could no longer perform his duties well, both mentally and physically. Churchill himself decided to retire in 1955. He was still a member of the Parliament though, until his retirement in 1964.

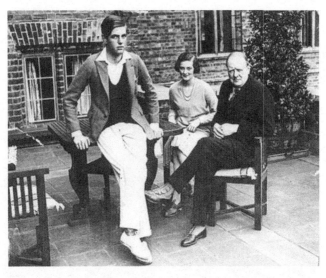

Churchill with his son Randolph (left) and daughter Diana (centre) in Chartwell House in an undated photo. (c) Daily Mail UK

As Churchill's health declined further, he was rarely seen in public. Many feared and assumed Churchill had Alzheimer's disease. However, his reduced mental capacity could only be attributed to the series of strokes that he suffered. Churchill was able to remain active in public life, despite his poor health. He also travelled and went on vacations with his wife. In 1960, for their 52nd anniversary, the two went to France and spent a month there.

In the autumn of the same year, Churchill suffered a fall while he was in his London home in Hyde Park Gate. He was admitted to the hospital in Paddington (St. Mary's) for treatment of a broken bone in his neck. Despite this, he was up and about again after three weeks.

Meanwhile, the US gave him an honorary US citizenship, a unique distinction only given to a chosen few, on

April 1963. Unfortunately though, their firstborn, Diana, committed suicide later that year.

After many other tours, vacations, and health scares, Churchill was not well enough to leave the house. As a result, their house in London was improved to accommodate him.

⫷ Death ⫸

Churchill suffered a severe stroke on January 15, 1965. He became gravely ill after this and died nine days later in his London home. He was 90 years old.

⫷ State Funeral ⫸

Queen Elizabeth II issued a decree on Churchill's death that his body lay in state for three days in the Palace of Westminster and a state funeral service was to follow at St Paul's Cathedral.

Churchill's coffin passed the Thames River from the Town Pier to Festival Pier in Havengore. It was reported that dockers had their crane jibs lowered

Churchill's coffin is carried down the aisle of St Paul's Cathedrla, 1965. (c) William Vanderson/Fox Photos/Getty Images via Huffington Post UK

in the form of a salute to honor Churchill. The coffin was then taken to Waterloo Station where it was loaded onto a railcar, specially prepared and painted for Churchill. The railcar was part of the funeral train that would carry Churchill to St. Martin's Church in Bladon. The Blenheim Palace, which was the official seat (house) of the Marlborough dukedom (his paternal grandfather was the 7th Duke of Marlborough), is under the parish of St. Martin's. Majority of the Marlborough family are buried there.

Because Churchill had served as head of government, he was given a 19-gun salute by the Royal Artillery. The Royal Air Force on the other hand, flew sixteen English Electric Lightning fighters in a fly-by.

During that time, Churchill's state funeral received the largest assembly of politicians and world leaders. While his funeral train carried his coffin, his mourners were transported through it as well. As the train travelled from London to Oxfordshire, thousands of mourners stood in the fields and on the streets to pay their last respects. In towns, some of the public stood and sat above buildings to get a better view.

✎ In Private ✎

To the world, Winston Churchill was an inspirational statesman, prolific writer, influential orator and credible leader. To his family however, he was a devoted husband and father. Churchill also loved having pets. He had hundreds of horses, several pigs, a parakeet, dogs and cats.

However, Churchill was most known for his lifelong habits of drinking and smoking. Of his drinking, many wanted to believe that he was abusive of his alcohol consumption. However, this was only a myth. He was not an alcoholic. If he were, he would not have accomplished what he did all those years.

Churchill was also a prolific writer. He had written 14 non-fiction books, two fictions, 28 compilations of speeches, and many articles for various newspapers and magazines throughout his career. In 1953, he was awarded with the Nobel Prize for Literature because of his accurate and excellent description of historical and biographical facts in his works. Aside from his writing, he also did paintings which he learned from his sister-in-law, Goonie. His family, at the initiative of Clementine, sold majority of his paintings when upkeep of the Chartwell House became difficult.

Sadly though, Churchill suffered from depression most of his life. He called it the "black dog" that continued to bother him until his old age. According to his daughter Sarah, depression left a void in his father's heart. His friend Lord Beaverbrook (Max Aitken, 1st Baron Beaverbrook 1879–1964) on one hand said that if Churchill was not in his best, confident self, he was at the bottom of intense depression.

To the world, Churchill is labeled in many ways. However, he is also known by his other names. People have dubbed him the British Bulldog, perhaps because of his bulldog-like scowl. William Manchester, historian and biographer, however, dubbed Churchill as the Last Lion in his books. To others, Churchill is simply, Winnie.

Conclusion

Churchill in Morocco, 1959. (c) Associated Press via Huffington Post UK

Churchill had versatility that was very rare not only in his time, but especially today. Of all his "hats" however, being a public figure was what he was best at. In public office, although he had mistakes, he did save and uplifted the British people and served as an inspiration for the rest of the world.

I hope this book was able to help you understand the life of Sir Winston Churchill, his achievements, and contributions to mankind.

Finally, if you enjoyed this book, then I'd like to ask you for a favor, would you be kind enough to leave a review for this book on Amazon? It'd be greatly appreciated!

Made in the USA
Las Vegas, NV
01 July 2022

50987030R10049